MW00957851

"Penn State: A Culture Designed to Crumble Under Pressure"

S.E.T. Culture: What Every Organization Needs to Know Before Crises Occur

"Morgan Stanley: A Culture Designed to Withstand Crisis"

Dr. Ken J. Brumfield

To my wife,

Your unwavering support and continued encouragement were invaluable through this journey and I am thankful for your sacrifices. I appreciate your daily advice and suggestions and your serving as my resident subject matter expert. My love for you is immeasurable.

To my sons,

Thank you for your love and support. Hopefully this book will inspire you to reach for your highest dreams and aspirations no matter what obstacles you may face. You all never cease to amaze me!

Acknowledgments

I cannot imagine going through this process without God and His ministering angels. I can truly admit that prayer is the key to dealing with life and its many challenges. I would like to acknowledge every individual who encouraged me along this journey. I would also like to thank Dr. Thomas Mierzwa, Dr. John - Sherlock, Dr. Kimberly Kelley, Mr. Keith Robertory, and Dr. Estella Lain.

Table of Contents

Chapter 1: Organizations in Crisis

"Sears Halts Sales of Firestone Tires After 21 Highway Deaths"
(*St. Louis Post Dispatch*, August 5, 2000)

"Colorado Scandal Could Hit Other Colleges"
(USAToday.com, May 26, 2005)

"Worst U.S. Shooting Ever Kills 33 on Va. Campus"
(MSNBC.com, April 17, 2007)

"83 Kinds of Toys Face Recall Over Lead. Fisher-Price Says They Were
Painted by Chinese Vendor"
(*St. Louis Post Dispatch*, August 2, 2007)

"Toyota Issues Recall of 550,000 Vehicles. News Comes on Heels of 18.5
Pct. Slide in Profit"
(*St. Louis Post Dispatch*, November 10, 2011)

"A Year Later, [BP Oil] Spill Still Defines State of Mind"
(*St. Louis Post Dispatch*, April 17, 2011)

"The Debt Crisis at American Colleges"
(*The Atlantic*, theatlantic.com, August 17, 2011)

Headlines in newspapers throughout the world herald company and
school crises on almost a routine basis. But their effects are far from routine. Such
crises — whether in business, education, or government or in for-profit or
nonprofit organizations — can dismantle the foundations and systems of
organizations: Top management may resign or, even worse, face imprisonment.
Middle management may be fired or demoted. Rank and file workers may be

1

laid off, often with no real hope of returning to their jobs. Stockholders lose money. The public loses confidence. And the average citizen affected by the precipitating event may suffer the most: lost wages, damaged property, personal injury – even death.

Business is well acquainted with crises that include a wide and ever expanding range of events: extortions, executive kidnappings, product recalls, industrial sabotage, copyright infringement, theft of proprietary information, work-related homicides, workplace bombings, terrorist attacks, and natural and man-made disasters. Routine daily operations no longer exist in organizations dealing with crises. Of most importance, however, is that crises can disrupt the perceptions of people in key leadership positions, causing them self-doubt and stress. The result is often the wrong decisions being made at the wrong time.

Effective crisis preparation and response are the keys to the viability of any organization. Yet many companies and schools are still not prepared for the inevitable. They have failed to take proactive steps to prepare for impending crises. By proactive, we're not talking about "how-to" approaches to crisis management. Numerous management approaches are currently being used in simulations, training, and seminars to assist leaders in effectively managing crises. Most of these programs focus on standard operating procedures (SOPs): lock-step procedures to be followed in an effort to avoid those "wrong

preparation + Respond!

2

decisions." But SOPs won't work in every situation. They may even make the crisis worse.

In *S.E.T. Culture: What Every Organization Needs to Know Before Crises Occur*, we're moving beyond the "how to" approaches. Our goal is to understand the underlying causes of successful and unsuccessful crisis management. Only by understanding the "why" behind successful crisis management will senior executives be able to establish organizational cultures that can weather crises and remain viable. In such organizations, management at all levels can make the right decisions to move the organization through the crisis as quickly as possible with the least damage to all parties involved.

Organizational Crises

What constitutes an organizational crisis? For our purposes, a crisis is any unplanned incident or event that negatively affects the viability of an organization. Crises are crises because they are perceived as being unlikely to occur. But when they do, the cause and ultimate effects of these high-impact events are ambiguous, leading to the presumption that "decisions must be made swiftly."[1]

Organizational Culture and Crisis Management

Researchers and emergency management consultants have studied and

---

[1] Pearson & Clair, 1998, p. 60.

3

evaluated crises at companies such as Firestone, Mattel, and Fisher-Price in the context of systems and contingency theories of management. But the culture of an organization is the critical factor in understanding its performance during a crisis. The strength and type of that culture determine how the organization adapts to change in its environment.

What is organizational culture? It's the dominant character of an organization: its values, beliefs, and behaviors. Over 200 definitions of organizational culture exist, each valid for the circumstances and the theory upon which it is based. For our purposes, Schein's definition encompasses the power of the senior executive team (SET) culture:

> a pattern of shared basic assumptions that was learned by a group as it solved its problems of external adaptation and internal integration that has worked well enough to be considered valid; therefore, it should be taught to new members as the correct way to perceive, think, and feel in relation to those problems.[2]

It is these assumptions and patterns of behavior, then, that managers and administrators fall back on during crises. However, many senior leaders fail to understand the effects of culture on their organizations and fail to use that culture to its full advantage.

Senior Executive Teams (SETs)

The SET is the highest management level within an organization. These

---

[2] Schein, 2004, p. 17.

leaders have responsibility for the day-to-day operations and, ultimately, the profitability of their company. Although a higher layer of executive power exists in the board of directors and shareholders, those groups are not involved in the day-to-day decisions that affect the way the organization carries out its mission and achieves its goals. The specific titles that comprise the SET may vary based on the type and size of the organization. Members of this team include the chief executive officer (CEO), chief operations officer, chief financial officer (or their equivalent titles in smaller organizations), and other upper level management appropriate to the specific company. Because of the wide variety in the number of individuals on the SET and in the specific positions those individuals hold within their organizations, in *S.E.T. Culture: What Every Organization Needs to Know Before Crises Occur*, we will simply refer to this group as the SET.

Individually, SET members have specific duties and responsibilities for the functioning of their offices, departments, or divisions. Collectively, they are responsible for the planning and decision making within the organization as a whole. SET members must embody two main characteristics:

1. They must be champions of their divisions or departments.

2. They must serve as senior advisors to the CEO.

They are the inner circle of executives who determine the strategic and tactical plans for their organization. These leaders must not only be willing to step

5

beyond their boundaries as senior division representatives to focus on the big picture or the overall vision and wellbeing of the company but also have the capacity to do so. *SET culture* is manifested as the CEO and the other senior executive cabinet members develop shared basic assumptions and beliefs.

SETs, Organizational Culture, and Crisis Management

When crises occur at the organizational level, any number of critical disruptions may occur. Companies may lose financial resources and key personnel. Infrastructure may break down. Continuation of normal operations may even be impossible. Consider these two examples of organizations in crisis:

- Firestone's major tire recall of Ford Explorers in 2000 affected not only Firestone but Ford Motor Company and its future growth. With 150 deaths and 1,100 accidents from high-speed blowouts caused by Firestone tires and combined costs of $10 billion for both companies, this one-time crisis has continued to have negative consequences for Firestone, its stellar image tarnished among consumers and other vehicle manufacturers.

- Mattel and Fisher-Price, in 2006, issued one of the largest product recalls in the history of the United States. Both companies encountered major crises when lead contaminants were discovered in their toys. The negative publicity surrounding the recalls resulted in major setbacks and challenges, including a $2.3 million fine imposed by the U.S. Consumer Product Safety Commission.

Educational institutions fare no better. Since 1999, educational institutions across the country have been affected by crises, beginning with the massacre at Columbine High School. Normal day-to-day operations in most schools have not been the same since. Consider these examples:

- The Virginia Tech massacre in 2007 left 32 dead and 25 wounded, not including the unknown psychological damage done to thousands of people both on campus and throughout the nation as a result of the intensive news coverage.

- In 2011, Joplin High School was struck by an E5 tornado, causing such devastation that the entire campus was declared irreparable. The school must be rebuilt from the ground up.

- Community colleges, universities, and other educational institutions have been particularly hard hit by the economy. Budget shortfalls and strained funding sources have resulted in staff and program cuts, school or campus closures, and no admittance to thousands of otherwise eligible students.

Such incidents have revealed the vulnerability of these institutions to both human and man-made disasters.

These examples show clearly that every type of organization must be prepared when, not if, a crisis occurs. But preparation goes beyond having enough insurance to cover the repercussions of disasters. Preparation goes beyond adopting a step-by-step crisis process. Real preparation for the crises none of us can predict requires understanding what the organization is, how it works, and how decisions are made within it. Real preparation means ensuring mid-level managers, those who report directly to SET members, are empowered to make effective decisions during times of crisis.

Mid-level managers have critical roles in times of crisis. Often the first responders in these situations, they must be prepared to act decisively. Their decisions may make the difference in saving lives and property, in retaining customers and organizational reputations, and in determining the life or death of their organizations once crises have passed.

The culture of an organization, particularly the SET culture, is what affects the decision making of these mid-level managers — and the SET is responsible for transmitting that culture. So, instead of just focusing on crisis planning, organizations may benefit from first analyzing and measuring their organizational culture in the context of crisis management.

Community Colleges: A Case in Point

Community colleges are a necessary component in the business and economic engine of the United States.[3] These public institutions of higher education are characterized by two-year curricula that lead either to associate's degrees or to transfers to four-year colleges. The College Board called them "indispensable to the American future . . . the Ellis Island of American higher education."[4] According to the American Association of Community Colleges, 1,175 community colleges exist in the United States and have a combined total enrollment of 12.4 million students.

Created to offer the benefits of higher education to all segments of the population, community colleges serve over half of the undergraduate students in the United States. These students view community colleges as economical, flexible, and well suited to their career and educational goals. In essence, community colleges allow people who cannot attend four-year colleges and universities to continue their education, build their skills, and advance in their careers. Community colleges advocate life-long learning, offering comprehensive educational programs to appeal to students of all ages, races, and socioeconomic backgrounds.

The missions of community colleges are similar to those of other

---

[3] Jenkins, 2008, p. 5.
[4] Ibid., p. 13.

businesses. Like other businesses, community colleges range in size, diversity, program variety, and urban or rural community focus. And just like other businesses, community colleges are not immune to critical disruptions and crises. They are experiencing increasing numbers of crises, ranging from ethics and discrimination violations to student unrest.

These institutions are currently being hit as hard by the economy as any other business, perhaps harder. Even though their enrollments are increasing rapidly, their financial resources are less and less certain as state and local governments cut funding to meet their budgets. In California, community colleges turned away over 140,000 students due to overcrowding.[5] In Salt Lake City, despite a 16% increase in enrollment, administrators had to close one campus because of severe financial cuts.[6] What applies to community colleges and other institutions of higher learning concerning managing crises applies to all businesses, regardless of size, mission, or location.

The Effect of Culture on Crisis Management Decision Making: The Model

Understanding the SET culture of an organization is the key to understanding and determining how mid-level managers will perform in crisis events. The model in Figure 1 shows the relationship of the various components

---

[5] Calareso, 2011.
[6] Chen, 2010.

involved. The underlying assumptions, espoused beliefs, and values—the cultural artifacts—of SET team members provide a snapshot of the SET culture and are the foundation for the type of SET culture that exists within the organization. This culture is also reflective of the culture of the organization as a whole. SET members pass this culture on to the managers who report to them. That culture affects the way these mid-level managers make decisions. Because mid-level managers play critical, even pivotal, roles during crisis events, their decisions affect the success or failure of their organization in surviving the crisis.

During crisis situations, managers usually make effective rational decisions when a balanced SET empowers and trusts them to manage the crisis. Mid-level managers usually make constrained decisions when a fragmented SET is distrusting and does not give them the authority they need to manage the crisis. Consequently, the SET culture does affect the way mid-level managers make decisions that, in turn, produce either successful (rational decisions) or unsuccessful (constrained decisions) outcomes.

The model is drawn from four main theoretical anchors:

- cultural dimensions of SETs in crisis management,
- management in the context of an organizational crisis,
- decision making, and
- leadership behaviors of SETs in crises.

11

These anchors are discussed more extensively in the next four chapters, with community colleges and other institutions of higher learning used to illustrate key points. We then look more specifically at the relationship between the components of the model to see the effect of SET culture on mid-level managers' decisions during crises and discuss the implications of this model for any organization.

Comprehending SET culture isn't the solution for all organizational performance issues, and understanding the decision making of mid-level managers won't solve every organizational crisis. But knowing how these elements interact will give SET members a different way of looking at their organizations, of analyzing their preparedness for any crisis situation, and of determining both changes that should be made to reframe the organizational culture and practices that should be reinforced within the existing culture to ensure success in the face of any potential crisis.

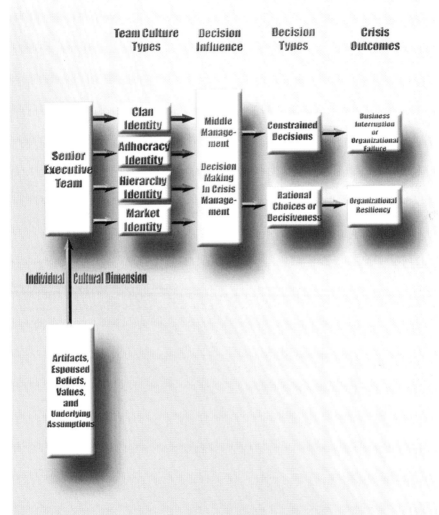

Figure 1. Effect of culture on crisis management decision making. Created by Dr. Brumfield.

13

Chapter 2: The Cultural Dimension

> Culture is a characteristic of the organization, not of individuals, but it is manifested in and measured from the verbal and/or nonverbal behavior of individuals—aggregated to the level of their organizational unit.
>
> Geert Hofstede

To understand the power of organizational culture, we must first look at what comprises culture. As noted in the previous chapter, hundreds of definitions exist for organizational culture, all of them valid in certain contexts.[7] Many of them include similar emphases: (a) shared values and beliefs that may be (b) consciously or unconsciously known by the leaders and members of the organization and (c) are used to guide the organization in attaining its goals and objectives and (d) the social behavior of those within the organization. Those shared beliefs and values shape the organization and give it meaning and direction. It's "how we do things here."

For our purposes, Schein's definition is most appropriate:

> a pattern of shared basic assumptions that was learned by a group as it solved its problems of external adaptation and internal integration that has worked well enough to be considered valid; therefore, it should be taught to new members as the correct way to perceive, think, and feel in relation to those problems.[8]

Elements of Organizational Culture

Researchers have developed a wide range of terminology to express the

---

[7] See Davis, 1985; Louis, 1985: Deal & Kennedy, 1982; Denison & Mishra, 1989; Dowty & Williams, 2011; Ouchi & Wilkins, 1985.
[8] Schein, 2004, p. 17.

elements of organizational culture, depending on the particular focus of their studies. Deal and Kennedy talk not only about values and norms that constitute a shared framework for successful goal attainment but also about myths, heroes, symbols, and artifacts as ways that culture is reinforced and taught to new members of the organization.[9] Basically, however, the culture of an organization—and how visible it is to an outside observer—may be discovered by examining three components within the organization: (a) artifacts, (b) espoused values and beliefs, and (c) basic assumptions.[10]

Artifacts. Artifacts are the surface behaviors and tangible, obvious items people encounter on a daily basis in an organization. They may be found in the casual observations people make: the way members interact with each other and with customers or clients, how they dress, the kind of language they use— anything easily discerned by people who are not part of the organizational culture. Viewed alone, artifacts may be misconstrued based on the biases of the observer, resulting in a skewed view of the culture. Instead, artifacts should be used in conjunction with the other two components to develop an accurate picture of the culture within the organization.

Espoused values and beliefs. Group members use espoused values and beliefs as a guide or a directional map to frame their behavior. Usually SETs look

---

[9] Deal & Kennedy, 1982.
[10] Schein, 2004.

to the president and other senior leaders for values and beliefs to guide the entire group. However, the group does not really share these values until they see them reflected in the actions of those senior leaders. Group members need to be convinced through positive actions before they will accept espoused values and beliefs.

Basic assumptions. These are the true values of the organization, which may or may not coincide with the espoused values and beliefs. Basic assumptions are the group's underpinnings, deeply seated ideas that exist beneath the surface of conscious thinking. Therefore, they are the greatest threat to the decision making of organizational leaders during crises because they are the most difficult part of culture to change.

Organizational Culture Typologies

Organizations are complex entities. Within them, more than one culture may exist. In *S.E.T. Culture: What Every Organization Needs to Know Before Crises Occur*, we are focusing primarily on the dominant culture of the organization, which is established by the SET. To discuss the effects of culture on decision making in organizations, we first have to determine the kind of SET culture that exists within the organization. Because the basic assumptions of an organization often reside below the conscious level of those within the company, various instruments have been developed to assess organizational culture and determine its dominant pattern of behavior.

One such instrument, the Organizational Culture Inventory, evolved from the instrument developed by Charles A. O'Reilly, Jennifer Chatman, and David F. Caldwell to assess the fit of individuals to specific organizations.[11] They identified seven dimensions through which the values of an organization may be determined. These dimensions provide a context for understanding how SET culture affects the decision making of mid-level managers:

- Dimension 1 (innovation and risk taking) is linked to the ability of SETs to push leaders beyond the status quo and out of their particular management comfort zones.

- Dimension 2 (attention to detail) entails SET members sharing the belief that innovation is a priority for the organization when facing a crisis. The entire organization establishes a mindset (and policies) that requires internal and external stakeholders to move beyond SOPs to seek alternative and unconventional methods for crisis management.

- Dimension 3 (outcome orientation) involves SETs being focused primarily on outcomes such as finished products and accurate delivery and on exceeding expectations.

- Dimension 4 (people orientation) is linked to the SET's focus on respect for

---

[11] O'Reilly, Chatman, & Caldwell, 1991.

personnel and valuing their contributions. People are not treated as widgets but as valuable assets to the organization.

- Dimension 5 (individual vs. team orientation) is focused on the contributions of a single team member versus the collective contributions of the team.

- Dimension 6 (aggressiveness) is the degree to which SETs push their leaders to make decisions in their favor.

- Dimension 7 (stability) is the degree to which an organization is willing to change or evolve.

The Organizational Culture Assessment Instrument is based on six dimensions: dominant characteristics of the organization, organizational leadership, management of employees, organizational glue, strategic emphasis, and criteria of success.[12] The intent of the instrument is to provide a snapshot of the existing organizational culture and a preview of the ideal culture for that organization.

Based on the results, organizations are identified as one of four dominant cultures: clan, adhocracy, hierarchy, and market (see Figure 2).

---

[12] Cameron & Quinn, 2005.

Clan (Collaborative)	Adhocracy (Creative)
Hierarchy (Controlling)	**Market** (Competing)

Figure 2. Dominant organizational culture classifications. Adapted from Kim S. Cameron and Robert E. Quinn, *Diagnosing and Changing Organizational Culture: Based on the Competing Values Framework* (Upper Saddle River, NJ: Prentice Hall, 2005).

Clan. This organization exemplifies the extended family. People within the organization are loyal and have a strong sense of commitment to the firm. Clan cultures focus on internal integration and orientation instead of external orientation. The primary goal is to concentrate on internal processes and organizational members. Mid-level managers influenced by clan culture tend to make decisions that are team-centered. Clan culture is also associated with successful organizational outcomes.

Adhocracy. An organization with this type of culture is flexible, adaptive, creative, entrepreneurial, and dynamic. The power within the organization may be constantly shifting from individual to individual depending upon the task. Adhocracy cultures are dedicated to entrepreneurism, innovation, and risk-taking. They are focused outwardly on competitive differentiation. This keeps the organization viable through shifting organizational strategies based on current conditions. Thus, adhocracy cultures influence mid-level managers to make decisions that are entrepreneurial, innovative, and risky in order to maintain organizational resiliency.

Hierarchy. In this kind of organization, the emphasis is on control, strict adherence to SOPs, rules, and policies. Most closely associated with a bureaucratic organizational structure, these organizations often have numerous layers of management and a high degree of control by top management. The organizational focus is usually internal rather than external, such as focuses on market and competition. Similar to clan culture, hierarchy culture concentrates on internal integration and orientation instead of external orientation. However, organizational members are not allowed to use much discretion in their decision making in such cultures. As a result, this culture is most often associated with organizational failure.

Market. The focus in this kind of organization is productivity and results, with the intent of being increasingly competitive in the marketplace. In market cultures, mid-level managers are expected to be determined, persevering, fierce competitors. Because the focus is on productivity and profitability, with an emphasis on increasing market share, this culture is associated with successful organizational outcomes.

Case in Point

The leadership teams of community colleges and other institutions of higher learning are usually composed of the president (or chancellor) and the president's cabinet. Although specific titles of the individuals in these positions may vary, cabinets usually include representatives of all major areas involved in the administration of the institution such as academic affairs, student life, research and technology, business and finance, faculty and staff, and marketing and public relations. The number of cabinet members varies with the scope and size of the college. As in other businesses, the president and cabinet are responsible to a higher level of authority, the board of trustees and, in the case of public institutions, local and state governmental agencies and the state legislature. However, the president and cabinet are responsible for the decisions made within the institution.

The SET exists within the cabinet. For some schools, the SET is synonymous with the cabinet. At larger schools or schools with multiple campuses, the SET is a smaller group within the cabinet. Other members of the cabinet may report to some of these SET members or may be elected representatives of faculty and student groups. Therefore, for our purposes, SET culture is confined to that established by the core group of leaders within the president's cabinet. These are the individuals responsible for crisis management during critical incidents.

In some community colleges, senior executives often serve in their capacities for extended periods, similar to executives of companies such as American Express where CEO Ken Chennault and his executive team have led the company through numerous challenges over the past nine years. In some institutions, these executives are given permanent appointments. When composed primarily of permanently appointed executives, SETS must be especially mindful of their influence on mid-level management, especially in crises. They must have a thorough understanding of not only the primary organizational culture but also the secondary cultures evidenced within the various units that comprise the institution.

On the other hand, executive turnover has also become quite common in businesses and in community colleges. According to the American Council on Education, the average tenure of college presidents is 8.5 years.[13] Turnover in these key positions is often due to securing higher positions at other institutions. The continually changing membership of SET teams in these institutions results in constant cultural shifts within the SETs. Such shifts may result in strain, tension, and incongruity within these organizations—all of which affect their ability to be proactive in planning for the inevitability of crises and to respond

---

[13] American Council on Education, 2010.

effectively to those crises.

Just as cultures vary from organization to organization, so too do the cultures of institutions of higher learning. Each campus within a multicampus system may evidence a slightly different culture even if all campuses reflect the overall belief structure of the system as a whole. Each department or group within an institution may also reflect a slightly different culture. Therefore, SETS need to understand not only the overall organizational culture of the institutional system as a whole but also the differences between campuses, departments, and groups to minimize cultural conflict. These SETS must also foster shared values, beliefs, and goals while respecting individual identities.

SETs in businesses and organizations that have multiple office locations, stores, plants, and distribution centers must also understand that they are dealing with multiple organizational cultures: the overall culture of values and beliefs established within the business and the cultures within each major segment of their business. Culture is affected by geographical location, size of the individual unit, and personalities of the leaders and employees. Yet all must embrace the overall organizational values, beliefs, and goals.

Xavier University: Exemplar of Adhocracy and Market Cultures

In 2005, Xavier University of Louisiana faced one of the most serious crises an institution can face: the devastating effects of Hurricane Katrina. Yet by

January 2006, the university was up and running once again. How did this institution manage not only to ensure its students and staff were safe but also to recover so quickly after the storm passed? Dr. Norman Francis, president of the university, and his SET used their collective experience to assess the situation through both adhocracy and market lenses and to empower their mid-level managers (i.e., campus police chief, director of housing, dean of academic affairs, facilities manager, registrar, director of operations, etc.) to make critical and significant decisions that saved student lives and determined the survival of this nationally prominent institution.

Unable to count on governmental agencies in the wake of Katrina, Francis and his staff used buses and boats to evacuate students and staff stranded on campus. Just weeks later, Francis "ordered up his own storm — of repairs, fundraising, and morale-boosting for the 4,000-student campus,"[14] culminating in the reopening of the university in January 2006. This nearly impossible feat was accomplished due to the combined adhocracy and market culture of the institution that allowed the SET to adapt to survive.

As noted previously, institutions embracing adhocracy cultures are flexible, adaptive, creative, dynamic, and entrepreneurial. They are dedicated to entrepreneurism, innovation, and risk-taking. They are also focused outwardly

---

[14] Clark, 2009.

on competitive differentiation to stay viable by shifting organizational strategies to meet current conditions. In this case, the SET knew that the longer the university stayed dormant and inoperable, the more students and faculty would begin to integrate into other universities and communities across the nation. They knew that the city of New Orleans needed this institution, "the most successful training ground for African-American physicians, scientists, and pharmacists,"[15] to be viable and healthy to assist with the massive rebuilding efforts taking place.

Although Xavier still struggles with the effects of Katrina and the economy, Francis and his SET have not only enabled the university to survive but also to thrive. Enrollment, which dropped significantly due to the devastation of Katrina, has steadily increased since then. In 2011, over 3,300 students were enrolled. Francis, his SET, and their empowered mid-level managers continue to improve facilities and to raise funds for scholarships to assist their students, most of whom require financial aid. They continue to improve existing curricula and design new programs to attract students. They continue to adapt to changing circumstances to achieve the mission of the university, the promotion of "a more just and humane society by preparing its students to assume roles of leadership and service in a global society."[16]

---

[15] Ibid., ¶ 2.
[16] "Mission," 2012.

Chapter 3: SET Culture and Risk Management

Risk is defined as anything that may disrupt the day-to-day activities of an organization or prevent planned activities, processes, or events from occurring. Risk management is "the total process of identifying, controlling, and eliminating or minimizing uncertain events that may affect system resources."[17] Many companies rely on a particular senior executive, often appropriately named the chief risk officer, to be aware of the various risks the organization may face and to comprehend their potential to affect the organization. Ultimately, however, the entire SET is responsible for creating a risk-aware culture. This includes understanding how their culture affects their managers' decision making during crises.

As a component of their strategic planning duties, SETS must create and maintain an integrative risk management framework to meet the heightened risk management expectations of shareholders and regulators. To do this, they must engage in effective two-way communication and prompt dissemination of risk information (e.g., potential threats). The entire organization, including all functional departments and units, must do the same. SET members should work with mid-level managers to create a culture consistent with Dimension

---

[17] Kovacich, 2003, p. 50.

1(innovation and risk-taking) and Dimension 3 (outcome orientation) from the Organizational Culture Inventory. During strategic planning, if senior leaders create and maintain an innovative risk management framework that involves risk taking, mid-level managers will be more likely to provide cultural attributes that support successful crisis outcomes.

SETs that use a risk management framework in their strategic planning also realize the following organizational benefits in mitigating risks:

1. A risk management culture is embedded throughout the entire organization based on upper management prioritization of risk management.

2. Policies, risk metrics and reports, and early warning indicators may be developed to complement the risk management initiatives.

3. Value is added to the organization through change management efforts, such as training in communications, risk-based performance management, and incentive programs.

Such programs are effective not only in managing risk but also in motivating employees to report potential threats and promote appropriate responses in a timely manner. A risk management organizational culture that supports and values input from internal and external organizational stakeholders is likely to experience successful organizational outcomes.

Risk Appetite

At the center of understanding the risk management culture of an organization is an understanding of its *risk appetite*, which is determined by the SET. There are two types or categories of risk, internal and external. Internal risks are incurred as part of normal daily operations. External risks are incurred outside of normal daily operations. How an organization defines its risk appetite dictates the way in which targets, strategies, and risk management are linked.

SETs who understand their organization's risk appetite can position their organization to be better prepared for a broader range of crises and to be more responsive to them whenever they arise.[18] Such organizational leaders may accomplish several efficiencies for their company:

- They can clarify the risks the organization is willing to assume.
- They can ensure their company properly articulates its risk appetite.
- They can ensure consistent communication to the various stakeholders of the overall plan for the strategy,
- They can implement tolerance metrics of their risk profile,
- They can prioritize organizational risks,
- They can develop new or revised policies and procedures.

---

[18] See Barfield, 2005.

Risk Strategy

The SET is also responsible for developing and implementing the risk strategy for their organization. Risk strategy is the actualization of the organization's risk appetite and the critical planning for mitigating the risks that the organization faces. Risk strategy is the link between general strategic principles and daily business activities. It is focused on opportunities while it minimizes the potential impact of any threats. This includes any value threats not consistent with Dimension 7 (stability). When SETs do not embrace this dimension, they are open to change yet are not willing to alter the aspects of their culture that hinder successful crisis management.

Case in Point

Community colleges and institutions of higher learning, like all businesses, must consider their risk appetite and develop risk management strategies. Although these institutions are subject to a diverse range of possible crises that vary in scope and intensity, the most pressing crisis facing these institutions presently is financial. Cutbacks in funding from both public and private sources, coupled with increased enrollments and costs, are causing the SETs of these institutions to develop severe financial exigency plans and to adopt budget cutting measures. At Houston Community College, a budget task force has been assembled "to balance a significantly reduced budget during difficult economic times while still maintaining the momentum"[19] the college has built over the past few years. However, in a report to the faculty, the task force also stated that dealing with the "'new normal' of reduced resources" is affording them the opportunity to "use this crisis to transform" the college.[20]

This college exemplifies the role of SET culture in risk management. Understanding that the probable reductions in funding will occur in the future, the college leadership team began four years earlier to take action to reduce the effects of decreased income. They involved their employees in generating cost-saving measures and revenue, resulting in a savings of over $15 million and additional revenue of over $1.4 million. They developed a team mindset to tackle the problem and encouraged "innovation, collaboration, and entrepreneurism"[21] to reduce costs, live within their budget, and find new sources of revenue so that the mission of the school would not be affected.

[19] Office of the Chancellor, 2011, p. 1.
[20] Ibid., p. 4.
[21] Ibid., p. 5.

Chapter 4: Crisis Management

> We sometimes emphasize the danger in a crisis without focusing
> on the opportunities that are there.
>
> Al Gore

The Institute for Crisis Management provides an annual detailed analysis of major crises, primarily those described in the news media that relate to management. In 2009, the majority (51%) of the crises reported were "management-related."[22] This suggests that managers and directors of organizations are doing a poor job of leading organizations through crises successfully, despite evidence that the repercussions of such crises may be severe.

But crises are not necessarily negative experiences for organizations. With appropriate planning and preparation and recognition of impending crises before they actually hit, crises can be used to the advantage of the organizations involved. One has only to remember that the Chinese character for "crisis" is a combination of the characters for "danger" and "opportunity" to understand the dual nature of these situations. Which side dominates is often a matter of the attitude and focus of the SET concerning crisis management.

---

[22] Institute of Crisis Management, 2010.

Crisis Management Teams

Crisis management is the systematic way in which members of an organization, in conjunction with external stakeholders, work to avoid potential crises and to minimize and resolve those that do occur. Some organizations have specific crisis management teams to deal with any organizational crisis. Other organizations rely on the SET to handle such situations. With either structure, the individuals involved must be capable of doing the job. They must be flexible and adaptable to continually changing conditions. They must be willing to listen to others and to share their own thoughts and ideas. They must be comfortable working in high-stress situations. The team must also be capable of responding quickly, decisively, and effectively.

Perspectives on Crisis

Inherent in effective crisis management is understanding the crisis from various perspectives. Without such understanding, leaders cannot ensure they are responding to the situation in the most appropriate way. Three basic perspectives exist in any crisis: the psychological perspective, the sociopolitical perspective, and the technological perspective.[23] In the psychological perspective, the crisis cannot be distinguished from the person who is actually experiencing the crisis. The focus is on the psychological outcomes of those individuals

---

[23] Pearson & Clair, 1998.

affected by the crisis. In the sociopolitical perspective, the crisis is the result of a "collective breakdown"[24] of the organizational culture. What once made sense no longer seems viable. In the technological perspective, the cause of the crisis is related to the interaction of technology with factors both inside and outside the organization. When technology, which is now essential in daily operations, functions properly, it affects organizations positively. However, when some aspect of technology malfunctions, interrupting major company processes, the results can be devastating.

Case in Point

Just as in other businesses, the overall responsibility for crisis management may be delegated to specific individuals or a team. However, ultimately the entire SET is responsible. The loose structure of most colleges means that a number of people from all segments of the college community will report to these leaders during the crisis. Therefore, crisis management leaders must have not only the skills and abilities to guide the college through crises but the respect of the college community in terms of both their character and the positions they hold within the leadership hierarchy. They must also have a thorough understanding of the organizational culture.

---

[24] Ibid., p. 64.

Unfortunately, community colleges and institutions of higher learning are also similar to other businesses in that they are less prepared to handle crises than they may believe they are. In a study of nineteen community colleges in Texas, the school administrators were found to be underprepared for crisis situations.[25] Even though an overwhelming majority of the respondents in the study stated that top leadership influenced appropriate personnel to develop crisis preparedness plans, few of these institutions had adequate plans for such critical events. Because organizational members such as community college deans and directors (i.e., mid-level management) are critical in deciding the crisis preparedness level in these institutions, the impact of the SET and its values and beliefs on the actions of mid-level management is clear.

Too often SETs fail to understand the need for preparedness until after crises occur. Because no plans exist, personnel scramble to contain the situations, often working at cross purposes. In some cases, SOPs are used to handle the situation, which, as discussed earlier, may or may not effect satisfactory results.

SETs and CEOs in these institutions also may not have a clear understanding of their specific organizational cultures. This lack of understanding affects leadership's ability to reduce the chances crises will occur, to be prepared when they do occur, and to ensure their institutions will survive

---

[25] Jenkins, 2008.

and thrive after crises pass. By understanding their existing cultures, these leaders—as well as SETs in any other kind of business—can strengthen their cultures and make them more supportive of the strategies devised for crisis management.

Responding to Crisis: Morgan Stanley

In addressing a Harvard Business School audience, Robert Scott, president and CEO of Morgan Stanley, said that little had prepared him for the events of 9/11.[26] However, he cited several factors that allowed the company, which was the largest tenant in the World Trade Center, to survive the disaster. Those factors included the company disaster contingency plan and well-trained managers. After the 1993 terrorist attack on the World Trade Center, Morgan Stanley had developed an evacuation plan and contingency plans for relocating their offices and creating a command center to continue operations. Because of those plans and the time leaders in charge of operations had spent drilling implementation of those plans, Morgan Stanley evacuated their people from the towers in the twenty minutes between attacks. When the second plan dove into what had been the company's retail security department, employees had already been evacuated. Of the 2,500 Morgan Stanley employees in the towers, only six

---

[26] Walsh, 2011.

were lost that day. Their backup site, located twenty-two blocks away, was activated by 9:20 a.m. that day; and by 9:30 a.m., senior management were relocated to a different backup site that served as the company's command center.

Scott cited several other actions taken during the crisis that have continued to benefit the company as a whole even after the crisis was over.[27] Most significant was the company decision to put the welfare of their people first, which resulted in revitalizing the company and giving it a new sense of unity and purpose. In fact, because of the single-mindedness created out of the disaster, 9/11 effectively cancelled the merger of Morgan Stanley with Dean Witter. Scott also noted the importance of working with people whose judgment he trusted: "You need good, able people in a crisis . . . and you need to make an investment in people long before a crisis ever hits. If you engender trust and loyalty, your people make it easier for you to lead."[28]

---

[27] Ibid.
[28] Ibid., ¶ 22.

Chapter 5: Decision Making in Crises

Individuals on the crisis management team need to be empowered to handle the situation and provided the resources to do so. SET culture is a determining factor in that empowerment and also affects the kind of decisions made during crises.

Managers must make decisions quickly during crises, often without sufficient resources, including information, on which to base those decisions. They may face numerous barriers beyond their control that distract them from making cogent decisions. Under such conditions, their decisions may be ambivalent or constrained rather than decisive. Ambivalent and constrained decisions increase the likelihood of negative outcomes for the organization. In this chapter, we look at organizational decision making, including various types of decision models, the role of ambivalence, and empowerment.

Decision-Making Models

Several models may be used within an organization in making decisions. Here we look at six:

- Model 1: Rational Choice
- Model 2: Bureaucratic
- Model 3: Carnegie and Bounded Rationality combined
- Model 4: Intuitive

- Model 5: Garbage Can

- Model 6: Ambivalence

Model 1. In the Rational Choice model, organizations use a rational process, usually a sequence of steps, to arrive at the best choice for the specific situation. During the process, organizational mid-level managers attempt to evaluate potential outcomes and possible consequences of various decisions that may be made to determine which one will resolve the issue in the best interests of the company. Mid-level managers who make rational decisions usually work collaboratively regarding their strategic direction and their intended accomplishments.

Model 2. In the Bureaucratic model, SOPs dictate decision making. The flexibility of managers is greatly reduced in this model under the guise of eliminating uncertainty in the process and in the decisions to be made. The result is constrained decisions.

Model 3. In this model, which considers the environment and circumstances in which crises may occur, two models are used in conjunction with each other: the Carnegie model and the Bounded Reality model. The Carnegie Model emphasizes the need for political coalitions in the decision-making process. Bounded rationality acknowledges "the limited resources at

38

disposal in the quest for information, along with the limited capacities of humans to discern such information."[29] In this combination, managers acknowledge limitations of both information and human discernment in the decision-making process.

Model 4. The Intuitive model is often used in organizations with "high velocity" environments, "those in which there is rapid and discontinuous change in demand, competitors, technology and/or regulation, such that information is often inaccurate, unavailable, or obsolete."[30] As a result of the fast pace and the numerous demands in this environment, mid-level managers tend to allow their emotions to guide their thinking. In other words, they "trust their guts" to make decisions. In some cases, doing so may impede sound judgment. Mid-level managers that base their decisions on emotional thinking and not rational judgment tend to produce bounded decisions.

Model 5. The Garbage Can model is often used by mid-level managers in ambiguous situations, those in which they have little information on which to base their decisions. Ideas, beliefs, goals, problems, solutions, values, myths—all are dumped into the "garbage can," allowing leaders to explore numerous possibilities before reaching a decision or series of decisions. Because everyone gets to put everything into the mix, this model may be best employed when

---

[29] Allen, Heidemann, Ingles, & Mills, 2003, p. 10.
[30] Bourgeois & Eisenhardt, 1988.

organizations are experiencing rapid, possibly unplanned, change and organizational goals are in flux.

Model 6. The Ambivalence model is "characterized by conflicted desires and approach-avoidance tendencies."[31] Simon illustrates this point by highlighting President Abraham Lincoln's ambivalence preceding the Civil War. Essentially, Lincoln faced a very tough decision: Use force or allow Confederate troops to entreat upon federal ground. Both options evidenced both enormous advantages and disadvantages. Lincoln decided to use force, the impact of which has lasted into the present day. Like Lincoln, mid-level managers are forced to make decisions and live with their ambivalence. Ultimately, what matters is that managers act decisively and are able to live with their decisions.

Various factors concerning organizational dynamics, such as communications and shared values, also affect the choice of decision-making models used within organizations. The level of interpersonal communication that occurs between the SET and mid-level managers is the key to the way in which any of the decision models are executed. Interpersonal communication is a "dynamic form of communication between two (or more) people in which the messages exchanged significantly influence their thoughts, emotions, behaviors,

---

[31] Simon, 2006.

and relationships."[32] For example, in the Garbage Can decision making model, if the SET and mid-level managers do not experience strong interpersonal communications, the managers will be more likely to make ambiguous decisions because the SET's thoughts, emotions, and behaviors will influence them.

Empowerment in Crises

Empowerment is essential to decision making. Webster states that empowerment involves giving legal authority to an entity. In the case of SETs, trusting mid-level managers with major decisions during crises is very important. The failure of SETs to empower their managers during crises can have a significant impact on their managers' decisions. When managers are not empowered to make decisions, they are more likely to allow the SET culture to determine their decisions. For managers to be empowered, decision making must be delegated and decentralized. The extent to which SETs are willing to relinquish power to their designated managers is the extent to which those managers will be empowered to act.

Empowerment is crucial in crises. Seldom do all members of the SET have expertise in all areas affected by the crisis. Seldom is information freely available during these critical events. Managers who may be closer to the "eye of the storm" are in positions to have the best available information and, thus, to make

---

[32] McCornack, 2007.

the most appropriate decisions. However, if they are not empowered to do so, if the SET has not trained them and given them the resources to make effective decisions in crisis situations, managers may feel constrained. As a result, they often make the decisions that they think the SET members would make. Those decisions may not be in the best interests of the organization in the long run.

Empowerment involves several stages of development. Conger and Kanungo identified four stages that one goes through before realizing that one is empowered to act.[33] In Stage 1, both mid-level managers and SET members must realize the lack of empowerment. Until SETS acknowledge that their managers are restricted from acting independently and the managers realize the extent of their actual power to make decisions, they cannot work to change the situation. Several factors contribute to the psychological powerlessness of managers: organizational factors, the enormity of the crisis, SET members' experience and training, stockholders' interests, SET members' involvement in the creation of the crisis, the nature of the job, rewards systems, and supervision.

Once this state and these factors have been acknowledged, SETS can employ various management strategies and techniques to increase involvement of managers in decision making and to build their skills in doing so. This is Stage 2. One way to achieve this is to conduct roundtable meetings between SET

[33] Conger & Kanungo, 1988.

members and mid-level managers to garner feedback, establish target goals, and create the plan for handling the crisis.

In Stage 3, SET members begin to build the self-efficacy of their subordinates. In this case, self-efficacy refers to mid-level managers' beliefs in their abilities to accomplish the tasks before them. SETS may employ various techniques to get their managers to see what they are capable of doing and the skills they have to accomplish the tasks at hand. Stage 3 is not about flattery or shallow compliments; it's about effective feedback and reinforcement of the skills and abilities needed to make effective decisions. In Stage 3, mid-level managers begin to feel empowered, to believe that they do have the skills necessary to perform appropriately during crises and to make the right decisions when there is no time to contact their supervisors for permission to act. In Stage 3, SET members often use their personal stories, virtual experiences, and their verbal abilities to persuade and to arouse emotion to help their managers attain the goals they have set in Stage 2.

In Stage 4, SETs continue to empower their mid-level managers, building within their managers a sense of performance expectation and personal efficacy. In this stage, mid-level managers realize they have been given not only the authority but also the skills to deal with emerging situations. They are empowered to make unconstrained decisions at the point of impact as the crisis unfolds to minimize negative effects.

SET Culture and Decision Making

The cultures that have a tendency to foster mid-level managers to make decisions resulting in organizational success or resiliency are the clan, adhocracy, and market cultures, as discussed in chapter 2. Mid-level managers influenced by the combined effects of adhocracy and hierarchy SET cultures tend to make crisis decisions that result in organizational success or resiliency. Mid-level managers influenced only by hierarchy SET cultures tend to make crisis decisions that result in organizational failure. Mid-level managers influenced only by Clan SET cultures to tend to make crisis decisions that result in ambivalent or constrained decisions. Keeping in mind that crisis events are intense and include high pressure internal and external elements and conditions.

Case in Point

In the context of community colleges, the effects of SET culture on decision making are similar. As in any business, the crisis management team must be trained to handle critical events. Then they must be given the power and authority to handle such events when they occur. When leaders are empowered with knowledge and crisis management strategies, they work more effectively in conditions of extreme stress and are more capable of making decisions under those circumstances. However, in institutions of higher learning, administrators

44

often do not clearly understand the effects of organizational culture on decision making. This can be detrimental during crises when decisions often must be made in a short time frame with limited resources based on incomplete information.

The response to the financial crisis at Houston Community College clearly demonstrates empowering mid-level management to lead during crises. In addition to a representative district-level budget task force, the chancellor authorized the creation of task forces at each of the six colleges in the system. Those college committees generated recommendations for budget cuts, revenue creation, and structural/organizational changes to reflect the new financial realities without compromising the mission of the institution. Their recommendations were given to the district-level committee, which studied the proposals, crunched the numbers, and made recommendations to the chancellor and board of trustees. As stated previously, this structure and the resulting recommendations are helping this institution not only weather the current financial crisis but also reorganize to achieve its mission more effectively and efficiently.

On the other hand, adverse, constrained decisions result when mid-level management are not empowered to act in crises, have no crisis management plan in place to guide them in their decision making, or fail to look beyond the obvious to consider additional possible scenarios. At Virginia Tech, university administrators' failure to notify students that the gunman who had just killed two people was still on campus resulted in additional deaths. The gunman attacked twice, first killing two students. The second attack did not occur until two hours later. Administrators, assuming the first attack was isolated, met an hour after the first shooting to determine how to notify students of the shooting. Although they had an email alert notification system and public address system, administrators had no real crisis management plan to guide them in decision making. Nor was a designated crisis management leader in evidence. Instead, the leadership team met to decide the appropriate course of action.

The first notification went out nearly ninety minutes later and only indicated the first shooting had taken place. A second notification went out approximately thirty minutes after the first, indicating the gunman was still on campus and directing students and personnel to lock down. This message, along with announcements over the public address system, was sent about ten minutes after police had entered the gunman's second location and found the gunman had committed suicide. The third notification cancelling classes occurred approximately fifteen minutes after the second message. Had officials cancelled classes immediately after learning of the first incident, fewer people may have lost their lives.

Virginia Tech is still dealing with the repercussions of these decisions. Although new protocols have been established that have been implemented several times since the 2007 massacre, they are indicative of reactions to crises rather than proactive crisis management planning.

Chapter 6: Leadership in Crises

If proper leadership is essential to good business, it is crucial during organizational crises. More important, proper leadership must be in place *before* the crisis arrives. Although numerous meanings and understandings of leadership exist, our focus is on leadership as a process of influence: over the organization as a whole, over specific aspects of the organization aligned with a leader's responsibilities, and over other members within the organization.

In responding to crises, organizations take their cues from their leaders. According to contingency theory, the context of the organization (SET culture) affects the effectiveness of leaders (mid-level managers).[34] Thus, whether these managers are ambivalent or decisive in making decisions is contingent on the SET culture within the organization. These managers are either limited and bound by the SET culture or released and empowered by it.

SETs provide vision and direction for their organizations. Those who are proactive focus on the future of their organizations; those who are reactive focus on what is occurring or has recently occurred. Reactive leaders address specific situations instead of anticipating and countering future issues before they can

---

[34] See Barnett, 2012.

become situations. Unfortunately, more often than not, SETS are reactive when it comes to crises.

To address defects latent in their SET culture, senior executives must be willing to take proactive steps to avoid mismanaging crises or experiencing unsuccessful crisis outcomes. They must be open to change. They must be willing to accept constructive feedback from their managers to develop a SET culture that empowers mid-level managers to make effective decisions during crises.

In the immediate aftermath of Hurricane Katrina, those businesses that quickly rebounded were led by leaders who refused to be distracted by insurance company and government red tape. This notion suggests there are characteristics inherent in leaders who successfully negotiate crisis situations. Innovative, decisive, and motivating leaders recognize that to move their organizations from crisis events to organizational resiliency, they must be willing to exhibit behaviors that support the cultural and value dimensions discussed in chapter 2, including risk taking and stability.

Senior executives who build effective crisis management skills begin by actively adhering to the environmental context and monitoring it. They actively seek to stay abreast of practices regarding crisis management. These leaders then support organizational preparation for potential crises, committing resources to doing so and increasing their mid-level managers' confidence in their abilities to manage crises effectively. It is important and comforting for mid-level managers to know that their SETs support crisis preparation activities. As the crisis unfolds, SETs and their mid-level managers react both individually and collectively to the situation. Both individual and collective actions are required in successful crisis response.

SETS also compare their actual responses in crisis situations to the planned responses of their organizations. They determine whether the organization followed its plan, whether the plan was actually appropriate for the specific situation, and whether adaptations were made to address short comings in the plan. They also assess whether the outcomes were positive or negative, successful or unsuccessful, which provides them with the information they need to rework their plans. Thus, SETs that manage crises effectively engage in a cycle of planning for crises, implementing those plans both to prevent and to navigate crises, and assessing both outcomes and processes to maintain appropriate levels of readiness for the next crisis.

Crisis Leadership

During crises, the normal leadership styles of SET members may not be sufficient to deal with the myriad facets of these situations. SET members must be able to perform under immense pressure and be decisive while maintaining their compassion and motivating the members of the organization to keep moving in the right direction despite the obstacles before them. To do this, they must be flexible with their leadership styles, adopting the styles required to enable their managers and other organizational members to deal with the crisis.

During crises, SET members need to be more visible than usual. Organization members need to know that the SET is there and is in control of the situation in order to do their jobs effectively. This is especially important because they may be called on to perform in ways they have not had to embrace before. SET members must also be especially effective communicators and negotiators, authoritative yet diplomatic.

SET members must be able to employ systems thinking, focusing not just on the evident problem but also seeing the potential effects of change in one component of the organization on the rest of the company. They must look beyond the immediate situation to focus on the root of the problem, expanding their evaluation of the situation to encompass both areas that may not yet be affected by the problem and long-term solutions. They must look for the interrelationships that exist within the situation, not linear cause-and-effect chains. Seldom are solutions to crises simplistic. SET members must look beyond simplistic answers to embrace real solutions.

Case in Point

Community colleges respond to internal and external crises, just as all businesses do. Although the nature of these crises may be different, their effects on the institutions and their stakeholders are very similar. Like other businesses, community colleges are also faced with global competition, competing for enrollment, funding, and resources with both other American and foreign institutions. In addition, they must compete with proprietary training institutions, which now offer similar degree programs.

These varied demands place tremendous strain on SETs and their mid-level managers, clearly illustrating the need for these leaders to embody the full range of leadership traits. These leaders must be flexible yet willing and able to make difficult decisions under intense pressure. They must be visionary and motivational, knowledgeable and decisive. They must plan, communicate, negotiate, delegate, and empower. They must be compassionate and diplomatic, responsive to all stakeholders. They must understand the potential effects of their decisions not just on the immediate areas impacted but also on the entire organization. That requires a thorough understanding of their organizational culture and the subcultures within their organizations. The extent to which these SETs take proactive approaches to address their cultural defects and position their organizations to experience successful crisis outcomes will directly impact

52

the ability of their institutions to rebound from crisis events.

Chapter 7: Towards More Effective Crisis Management

Every organization is susceptible to a host of crises, from natural disasters to terrorist threats to unforeseen economic conditions. The culture of the organization, especially the SET culture, determines to a large extent how successfully the organization will resolve crises and how likely the organization will continue as a viable entity. To illustrate this, let's look at two examples, one showing the positive effects of creating a culture that enables the organization to withstand crises and one showing the ramifications of not doing so.

The U.S. Coast Guard: A Culture Designed to Withstand Crisis

Images of the aftermath of Hurricane Katrina may be forever etched in the memories of millions of people across the world. Avoiding media coverage of the elderly and disabled suffering along Interstate I-10, interviews with survivors trapped in and around the Superdome, the devastation, and the fear of residents not knowing when — or if — they would be rescued or whether they could recover from losing everything they had was nearly impossible. Hurricane Katrina dealt devastating human, financial, and structural blows not only to metropolitan New Orleans but to the entire Gulf Coast region. And the response from most local, state, and federal officials and agencies was poor at best. Yet, amid the negative criticism aimed at all levels of government, the Coast Guard displayed exemplary performance in their rescue and recovery efforts.

The motto of the United States Coast Guard is *semper paratus*, "always ready." Never was this more apparent than with Hurricane Katrina. Admiral Robert Duncan, head of the Eighth District headquartered in New Orleans, was charged with dealing with this epic storm. He ensured that the appropriate vessels, including cutters and helicopters, were dispersed before the storm hit. He requested additional manpower from the Fifth District to handle the crisis. As a result, some 1,200 lives were saved before the Federal Emergency Management Agency (FEMA) ever arrived on the scene.

The Coast Guard was able to act and react with such speed and effectiveness because of its organization. Each geographic district has its own command and control center and is empowered to act autonomously to meet whatever situations arise. Commander Richard J. Dein USCG retired, reiterated this point to the Association of Contingency Planners, stating, "We don't have to get approval to execute."[35]

Thus, the Coast Guard exemplifies an *adhocracy culture*, which is synonymous with being flexible, adaptive, and responsive to external conditions. The autonomy for each district to respond as needed to meet the specific

---

[35] Striedl, Crosson, & Farr, 2006, p. 8.

situations in their geographic area allowed Admiral Duncan and his SET team to address the crisis created by Katrina effectively and efficiently. They, in turn, allowed their mid-level managers to make decisions that ultimately saved lives and property. This "response ready network" exemplifies the organizational structure and SET culture needed to make the right decisions during times of crisis.

Penn State: A Culture Designed to Crumble Under Pressure

The recent and ongoing crisis at Penn State University involving Jerry Sandusky and the child molestation scandal illustrates what happens when the SET culture does not allow for effective crisis management. The dominant Penn State SET culture prior to the crisis was the *clan* culture. Clan cultures are characterized by closely knit family bonds, including the tendency to protect family members or cover up another member's secrets or mistakes, which is exactly what happened at Penn State. SET members Gary Schultz, vice president for finance and business, and Tim Curley, athletic director, covered up the allegations related to Sandusky and either ignored or failed to respond appropriately to allegations that wrongdoing was occurring or had occurred. According to ESPN, Schultz, who oversaw the campus police, "never reported the 2002 allegations to any authorities." In their report, the grand jury investigating the case stated that Schultz "'never sought or received a police report on the 1998 incident and never attempted to learn the identity of the child in the shower in 2002.'" Even more important, the grand jury noted that "'no one from the university did so.'"[36] That included Joe Paterno, head football coach and mid-level manager, although he was not implicated by the grand jury in any wrongdoing.

Paterno had technically followed school policy by reporting the sexual allegations to university administrators.[37] He did not contact police, however, and did not initiate any other form of follow up. This despite stating that the assistant coach who reported the allegations to him had been visibly upset. Because he had not given Paterno the specific details that were later given to the grand jury and because Sandusky was retiring from the coaching staff, Paterno simply referred the allegations to university officials. In effect, he too looked the other way, exhibiting classic clan culture.

Although Clan cultures have the tendency to produce organizational success, the SET Clan culture at Penn State resulted in Paterno and others making decisions that produced negative and unsuccessful organizational outcomes. The final impacts of this crisis, which so far has resulted in criminal investigations, terminations, lawsuits, and the tarnished reputations both of the

---

[36] ESPN.com News Services, 2011.
[37] Ibid.

university and of what had traditionally been a stellar sports program, may not be known for years. Of most importance, however, is that this SET culture harmed the very people the university was supposed to nurture and protect, the students.

Applying the Model

SET members share their beliefs and pass them on to new members as the organization responds or adapts to changes in external and internal conditions, in our case, crises of various kinds. During this adaptation process, SETs teach new members the correct way to perceive, think, and feel in relation to crises, thus providing direction for their organizations. As reflected in our model (Figure 1), different types of SET culture influence mid-level managers' decision making in unique ways.

SET and organizational cultures may be classified into four different types: clan, adhocracy, hierarchy, and market. These cultural types influence SET members and mid-level managers to make certain types of decisions in crisis situations: constrained or rational. Rational decisions lead to organizational success after crises. Constrained decisions lead to organizational failure.

Although SET members usually have specific roles they are to execute during crises, they may not have the skills or experience necessary to perform them effectively and efficiently. Several studies have shown that SET members may be underprepared or may not have adequate plans to address crisis situations. Managers may be faced with numerous barriers beyond their control that distract them from making cogent decisions. As a result, they cannot make decisions that are sound and beneficial for the organization. Instead, their decisions are often ambivalent or constrained.

Thus, we can clearly see that the following are true, as reflected in the model:

1. SET cultural values tend to influence the culture of the organization.

2. In balanced and trusting SET cultures, managers are effectively prepared to oversee crises.

3. A balanced and trusting SET causes their managers to employ systems thinking when facing crises.

4. In fragmented and distrusting SET cultures, managers tend to make constrained decisions in crises.

5. When SETS and mid-level managers are effectively prepared to manage crises, successful outcomes usually result.

6. When SETs empower their managers during crises, organizational outcomes tend to be positive.

To develop more effective crisis management, organizations must discuss crisis management in earnest, beginning with their senior leadership tier.

Taking the Next Step

Businesses must find a balance between participating in continuity planning and allocating resources (labor and other expenses) to do so and focusing on their viability after crises. No organization can anticipate every crisis. However, acknowledging that crises may occur and developing crisis management plans to implement during such events are not enough. Organizations must take these steps to ensure they will be resilient and successfully survive any crisis:

1. Develop an understanding of their SET culture.

2. Prepare all management for their specialized roles during crises.

3. Empower mid-level management to make rational decisions during crises.

Developing an understanding of organizational culture. Businesses must have a clear understanding of their organizational culture, the SET culture, and its effects on decision making within the organization. Individual SET members possess various personal attributes, beliefs, and values that contribute to the collective SET culture. These shared values determine how leaders influence their mid-level managers' decision making and react to their decisions.

To do this, SETs should consider administering one of the organizational culture inventories available, such as the Organizational Culture Assessment

Inventory. With this information, SETS will see the congruence between the SET culture and between the various subcultures within the organization. SETS can use that information to address the problems within the culture that may result in ambivalent, constrained decisions, inaction, or adverse decisions on the part of mid-level managers when crises do arise.

Becoming aware of what currently exists is the first step in altering and changing individual and team cultural attributes that are counterproductive to successful crisis management. Developing an awareness and understanding of the SET culture within an organization will allow leaders to be better prepared for overall crisis management, to select and hire appropriate top and middle management personnel, and to improve strategic organizational planning. Mid-level managers may also understand their own decision-making processes better, and improve their performance during crises.

Preparing all management for specialized roles. Business must go beyond surface preparedness and business impact studies to ensure that SET members and all management are thoroughly prepared for the specialized assignments they must handle during crises. Although these roles may be embedded in their job descriptions or explained in the detailed crisis management plan, they may involve skills or processes that SETs and mid-level managers do not use on a regular basis. To ensure that crisis management is carried out as smoothly as possible, all SET members and mid-level managers that must take on responsibilities outside their normal duties should receive on-going training in these skills and processes. Failure to do so will result in crisis plans that look good on paper but have little chance of being successfully implemented. Success can be ensured only to the extent that all individuals in leadership positions understand their unique roles in crisis situations and have the skills and abilities to carry out those roles.

Empowering mid-level managers. Businesses must ensure that mid-level managers are empowered to make rational decisions during crises without having to consult SET members. These managers often face challenging situations during crises. They must have the skills and authority to act to minimize any negative effects on the organization. In crises, little time may exist for consultation with top leadership, who are usually far removed from the immediate situation. Therefore, mid-level management not only must be given authority to act but also must believe that they do have such authority. Failure to do both may result in constrained management decisions, which lead to adverse crisis outcomes, including loss of life, property, and financial resources.

The Power of Understanding SET Culture

Our goal in this book, as we said in chapter 1, is to understand the underlying causes of successful and unsuccessful crisis management.

Corporations, small businesses, community colleges, nonprofit institutions — all organizations face crises. By understanding how SET culture affects decision making within the organization, senior leadership can ensure that all individuals in the organization know and understand their roles in crisis management. They can empower their managers to make the right decisions during such times, minimizing adverse consequences. Senior leadership can build the kind of culture that will allow their businesses to weather any crisis successfully.

Bibliography

Allen, M., Heidemann, E., Ingles, B., & Mills, J. (2003). Putting organizational theories to test: An explication of William-Langewiesche's *American ground: Unbuilding the World Trade Center*. Retrieved from http://teachpa.appstate.edu/2004_TeachPA_conference /Allen

American Council on Education (2010). *American college president*. Retrieved from http://www.acenet.edu/Content/Navigation Menu/ProgramServices/CPA/Executive_Summary .htm

Barfield, R. (2005, January). Risk appetite — How hungry are you [Special risk management edition]. *The Journal*. Retrieved from www.pwc.com/gx/en/banking-capital-markets /pdf/risk_appetite.pdf

Barnett, T. (2012). Leadership theories and studies. In *Reference for business. Encyclopedia for business* (2nd ed.). Retrieved from http://www.referenceforbusiness.com/management /Int-Loc/Leadership-Theories-and-Studies.html

Bourgeois, L. J., III, & Eisenhardt, K. M. (1988). Strategic decision processes in high velocity environments: Four cases in the microcomputer industry. *Management Science, 34*, 816–835.

Calareso, J. (2011, February 18). Community colleges in crisis. *Education Insider News Blog*. Retrieved from Education Portal.com: http://education-portal.com/articles/Community _Colleges_in_Crisis.html

Cameron, K. S., & Quinn, R. E. (2005). *Diagnosing and changing organizational culture: based on the competing values framework*. Upper Saddle River, NJ: Prentice Hall.

Chen, Grace (2010). *Budget crisis 2010: Will community colleges be declared financial emergencies*. Retrieved from http://www.communitycollegereview .com/articles/212

Clark, K. (2009, October 22). Norman Francis: Xavier's president led through Hurricane Katrina, *U.S. News*. Retrieved from http://www.usnews.com/news/best-leaders/articles /2009/10/22/norman-francis-xaviers-president-led-through-hurricane-katrina

Conger, J., & Kanungo, R. N. (1988). The empowerment process: Integrating theory and practice. *Academy of Management Review, 13,* 471–482.

Daft, R. L. (2007). *Organizational theory & design* (9th ed.). Cincinnati, OH: South-Western College Press.

Davis, T. (1985). Managing culture at the bottom. In R. Kilmann, M. Saxton, & R. Serpa (Eds.), *Gaining control of the corporate culture.* San Francisco, CA: Jossey-Bass.

Deal, T. E., & Kennedy, A. A. (1982). *Corporate cultures: The rites and rituals of corporate life.* Harmondsworth, England: Penguin.

Denison, D., & Mishra, A. (1989). Organisational culture and organisational effectiveness: A theory and some preliminary empirical evidence. *Proceedings of the Academy of Management, 168*–172. Available from Denison Consulting: http://www.denison consulting .com/dc/Portals/0/Docs/Paper_cult_eff.pdf

Dowty, R., May, P. J., Beech, C. E., & Wallace, W. A. (2011). Organizational culture and the Katrina response in Louisiana. In R. Dowty & B. Allen (Eds.), *Dynamics of Disaster: Lessons on Risk, Response, and Recovery* (ch. 2). London, England: Earthscan.

ESPN.com News Services. (2011, November 7). *Penn State AD, school VP leave posts.* Retrieved from http://espn.go.com/college-football/story/_/id7201952/penn-state-nittany-lions-tim-curley-takes-leave-gary-schultz-steps-amid-scandal

Institute of Crisis Management. (2010). *ICM crisis report: News coverage of business crises during 2009.* Louisville, KY: Author.

Jenkins, M. (2008). *Exploring factors influencing crisis preparedness among Texas community colleges with residential students* (Doctoral dissertation). Northcentral University, Arizona. Retrieved from Dissertations & Theses: Full Text. (Publication No. AAT 3338718)

Kovacich, G. (2003). *Information systems security officer's guide: Establishing and managing an information protection program.* Burlington, MA: Elsevier.

Louis, M. R. (1985). Perspectives on organizational culture. In P. J. Frost, L. F. Moore, M. R. Louis, C. C. Lundberg, & J. Martin, *Organizational culture* (pp. 27–29). Beverly Hills, CA: Sage.

McCornack, S. (2007). *Reflect and relate: An introduction to interpersonal communication.* Boston, MA: Bedford-St. Martin's Press.

Mission. (2012). *Quick facts.* Retrieved from Xavier University of Louisiana website: http://www.xula.edu /mediarelations/quickfacts.php

O'Reilly, C. A., Chatman, J., & Caldwell, D. F. (1991). People and organizational culture: A Q-sort approach to assessing person–organization fit. *Academy of Management Journal, 34,* 487–516.

Office of the Chancellor. (2011). *Budget task force report* (No. 2). Houston, TX: Houston Community College. http://www.hccs.edu/System%20Home/Departments/Chancellor /Budget%20Task%20Force/Budget%20Task%20Force%20Report%202.pdf

Ouchi, W. G., & Wilkins, A. L. (1985). Organizational culture. *Annual Review of Sociology, 11,* 457–483.

Pearson, C. M., & Clair, J. A. (1998). Reframing crisis management. *The Academy of Management Review, 23*(1), 59–76.

Schein, E. H. (2004). *Organizational culture and leadership* (3rd ed.). San Francisco, CA: Jossey-Bass.

Simon, A. (2006). Leadership and managing ambivalence. *Consulting Psychology Journal, 58*(2), 91–105.

Striedl, P., Crosson, J., & Farr, L. (2006). *Observations of Hurricane Katrina lessons learned.* Albany, NY: Association of Contingency Planners.

Tharp, B. M. (2009). *Four organizational culture types* (Organizational Culture White Paper 4). Haworth. Retrieved from http://haworth.com/en-us/Knowledge/Workplace-Library/ Documents/Four-Organizational-Culture-Types_6.pdf

Walsh, C. (2011). *Leadership on 9/11: Morgan Stanley's challenge.* Retrieved from Harvard Business School Working Knowledge for Business Leaders Archive: http://hbswk.hbs .edu/archive/2690.html

Made in the USA
Charleston, SC
18 June 2012